What I
About C

101 Observations

By Liv Hambrett

Illustrations by Josh Bauman

Published by:
epubli GmbH, Berlin, www.epubli.co.uk

ISBN 978-3-8442-7278-9

Introduction

Münster came first, a neat, pretty city with a disconcertingly large bicycle population and a marked distaste for small talk. I flapped and flailed for a while before – sort of – getting the hang of the very precise manner in which the Münsteranians do things. Just as I was getting really good at not jaywalking and not engaging bus drivers in chit chat, I was whisked away to a tiny town in Bayern, tucked away in the Oberpfalz. In Weiden people said "Hi" to each other on the street and I probably would have fit in pretty well with their overall jolliness if I could have understood a word they were saying in Oberpfälzisch. And then came Kiel, a city full of those famously aloof northerners who proved to be the friendliest (and most direct) of the lot.

In both cities and that little town, I zealously collected data in between sampling every single type of cheese, chocolate and Schnitzel available to me. The German people, an enigma when I first arrived in Düsseldorf on a grey,

rainy afternoon, began to come into sharp relief. A little bit strange, a little bit strict – but warm and fun and wonderfully forthright.
In an effort to share what I had found about these people, What I Know About Germans was born. What follows is a list compiled with great love and a drop of generalisation, developed over my time spent living here as a rule-breaking, small-talk-loving, snow-hating Australian.

Germany, I know how you feel about the excessive use of the word "love" and I know that right now you'd rather shake my hand. But I love you. Give me a hug.

Liv Hambrett

1.

Germans are tall.

2.

Germans enjoy dairy products (this may have something to do with their height). The refrigerated sections of their supermarkets are homages to experimentations with yoghurt and quark. They will put a cheese- or cream-based sauce with most things.

3.

Sauerkraut is both enjoyed and oft consumed, as per the universal expectation.

4.

But the cabbage thing doesn't stop there. Both Krautsalat and Rotkohl are regular meal (and doner kebab) companions, the latter readily available in the frozen section of any local supermarket.

5.

Germans have really embraced the organic food trend and dedicate supermarket shelves to products emblazoned with "BIO".

6.

Germans enjoy frozen vegetables.

7.

And Spargel. They love asparagus and anything to do with asparagus, like Spargel peelers and Spargel steamers and Spargel platters. Forget Christmas or Easter or any other notable markers, the German year revolves around Spargelzeit.

8.

Germany has assumed the doner kebab as a national dish, Germanified it with pickled cabbage and elevated it to where it now sits, loftily, alongside other key German snacks like Currywurst and Fischbrötchen.

9.

Germans have excellent winter wardrobes (perhaps because German winters are endless).

10.

They lose their shit when the sun comes out. They flock to outdoor cafes and tip their faces to the sun... but remain in boots and jeans with a pashmina close by. Even when it's 25 degrees. Even when it's obvious the weather isn't going to turn. Because...

11.

...Germans are always prepared for the rain.

12.

Germans are very good bike riders – nay, they are exceptional bike riders. They manage to look elegant while freewheeling down cobbled streets, pashminas blowing out behind them. They are also highly adept at riding with umbrellas.

13.

Thus, German kids learn to ride young. They start in small wagons attached to their parents' bicycles and move through the ranks until, at six years old, they are fully-fledged members of the cycling community.

14.

Their babies are particularly beautiful.

15.

Germans are punctual. It's in their genetic make up. They cannot be late.

16.

In fact, they place an enormous premium on the three Ps – Practicality, Punctuality and Planning.

17.

Germans are rather thrifty and don't have the weird Anglo qualms with talking about money...

18.

Germans can eat. And drink. A lot. They have excellent constitutions.

19.

And they can always enjoy a Bratwurst, no matter the time, no matter the place. And they never seem to drip the sauce all over themselves.

20.

Germans love meat. In all its incarnations. Raw, fried, crumbed and dripping in mushroom sauce. But mostly, processed and stuffed into stomach lining.

21.

They worship the pig. He is revered as both a lucky (Glücksschwein) and delicious little fellow in this country and there is no part of the pig that cannot be boiled, shredded, fried, processed, mashed, diced and consumed. And there is no end to the various pig likenesses that can be crafted from marzipan.

22.

Germans speak English better than most English people. Or at least they get "there, they're and their" correct every time, which is more than many native English speakers can say.

23.

They are good at mostly anything they do. Or, if they're not, they try hard and become competent. Because...

24.

...Germans are thorough. They seem to live by the "do it once and do it well" principle. They work hard and effectively, despite working some of the shortest hours in the Western world.

25.

Consequently, Germans have the strongest economy in Europe. What they do during those short hours is probably double what every other country manages in twice the time.

26.

For many Germans, the weekend begins at 1pm on Friday afternoon. The week's work has been done and done well and now it is time to enjoy the spoils of a well-spent weekend.

27.

If a study were done on how well different nationalities dance in a club or bar situation, Germany probably wouldn't be in the top ten for general skill. But would they would absolutely ace the enthusiasm component.

28.

Germans are not afraid to whip out the smoke machine on the dance floor.

29.

They have an unexpectedly wicked sense of humour. David Hasselhoff, anyone?

30.

...a man they continue to celebrate by playing "Looking for Freedom" far more than any other country.

31.

After all, they embrace one hit wonders. Royalties from German radio single-handedly keep the singers the rest of the world wants to forget in rent money.

32.

Germans can have entire conversations that consist solely of the word "doch".

33.

Germans love a good boot.

34.

And they never scuff them. Even when bike-riding down a cobbled street in the rain, holding the shopping and an umbrella, pulling a wagon behind them with a child contained within.

35.

Germans, largely, are always exceptionally well groomed.

36.

They simply do not understand flip flops as viable footwear. Even when it's warm and sunny, and a boot is impractical or too warm for the feet to be comfortable. Outside of a very small, very obviously summer, window they will stare, bewildered, at thonged feet and quietly wonder if the wearer is mad.

37.

Germans struggle enormously with the concept of "naked feet". It is better feet be clothed at all times.

38.

Maybe that's why there are more instances

of socks paired with sandals in Germany than in other countries.

39.

Germans are refreshingly comfortable with nudity. The further east you go, the more apparent this becomes.

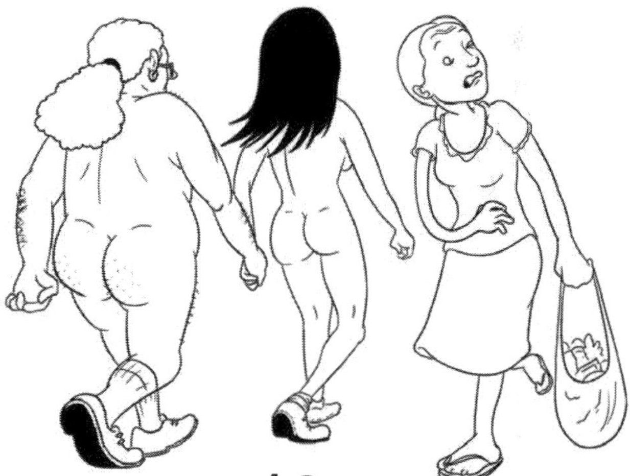

40.

Should a contestant on a family-friendly "celebrity special game show" be a nude model, German TV is totally down with displaying a great deal of her portfolio, to the audience at home. Before 9pm.

41.

Germans are generally very open and relaxed about most things sex-related. They are a candid, frank people.

42.

German men don't tend to leer.

43.

But, Germans stare. Not in a way designed to be particularly rude, but in an unabashed, piercing, inquisitive way that makes you wonder if you have food on your face or your skirt is tucked into your underpants.

44.

They love a large, mind-bogglingly well-stocked hardware store (with a Bratwurst stand out the front). Perhaps because another mantra of the Germans could be, "if you want something done well, do it yourself".

45.

Germans have bottomless basements.

46.

Germans are very fair people and adhere to regulations that exist to keep things fair for the masses.

47.

This works because Germans love a good rule. And they reap the benefits of a rule-abiding society.

48.

They don't appreciate the use of the rude finger when driving. If you give it to a fellow driver, that driver reserves the right to report you and your licence plate, and you will get a fine.

49.

Germans don't jaywalk. And they judge those who do with a piercing, back-burning gaze.

50.

Collectively, German people seem to have a very sweet tooth and the cake, biscuit, chocolate, sweets aisles of their supermarket are of Willy Wonka proportions.

51.

Germans love doing Kaffee und Kuchen for all sorts of occasions.

52.

They love the breakfast meal and fill the table with four different types of cheese, five different types of meat and a basket of bread rolls.

53.

Germans. Love. Bakeries.

54.

As a general bread rule, they seem to enjoy a darker or seeded bread. Or at least bread with a long name that nods to exciting contents.

55.

Germans aren't big on bread slicing.

Sliced bread, or "toast Brot", is relegated to the toaster and sandwiches made with sliced bread enjoy a disproportionately small section of the bakery display in comparison to their friends, the Brötchen.

56.

Germans can open a beer bottle with anything. The couch, a coffee mug, a banana. Body parts. It's like they all secretly take a class at school when they're 11, in preparation for a lifetime of beer consumption.

57.

Germans can drink. And not just write themselves off, vomit in the bathtub at 2am, wedge in a kebab and back it up the following night, à la Australian/ English/ American binge drinkers... but drink. While the rest of the world is vomiting in the bathtub, the Germans are calmly ingesting their 24th shot and washing it down with a beer, their cheeks a little rosy, their eyes a little glazed, but their livers working as smoothly as a German-made automobile.

58.

This is because Germans start drinking young. They are allowed to drink "soft alcohol" (beer and wine) at 16 and "hard alcohol" (sprits) at 18. By the time kids from other countries are losing their shit with alcopops, the Germans are enjoying a much more tempered relationship with alcohol... and the benefits of a much more match-fit liver.

59.

Germans do not suffer fools gladly, thus only putting up with drunk Australians and Americans during Oktoberfest because we'll pay hideous amounts of money for hideous amounts of beer.

60.

They don't necessarily say it to your face, at the time... but Germans don't like it when you go against the tide in the supermarket...

61.

...or get on the bus through the wrong door. This they will say to your face, using a microphone and an unimpressed tone.

62.

Germans can't queue. They don't know how, they have no interest in trying. This is the one time Germans embrace a lack of system, and what happens when a queue is called for is the unfortunate culmination of Germanic forcefulness and uncertainty in the face of a system-less world.

63.

Take, for example, what happens in a supermarket when another check out line opens. Instead of calmly indicating to the person at the top of the queue, yet to unload their basket onto the conveyor belt, that they should head up the new checkout line, there is this mad dash like a scattered flock of sheep, and one's standing in the original queue becomes completely irrelevant. If you are fast enough, you can theoretically come from well behind and end up getting served before the person five people in front of you. And no one thinks anything of it.

64.

Germans have the single most nerve-wrackingly rapid supermarket checkouts in the world.

65.

They are not ones to make small talk at the supermarket checkout. Or in general, really. Words without purpose are wasted words.

66.

This is because Germans are generally extremely direct people. They do not see a need for conversational subtext. They say it as they see it, while keeping you at the appropriate arm's length distance. Directness and distance are valued social commodities.

67.

Apropos, Germans will always try and shake your hand, even if you feel you've reached the status of hugging.

68.

But when you crash through those notorious barriers, you have a German pal for life.

69.

Germans love Dakels (dachshunds) and seem to own several of them at once. Perhaps this adoration of dachshunds stems from their physical similarity to Wurst.

70.

In fact, Germans love all dogs. Often their dogs catch the bus with them and sometimes their dogs even dine with them in restaurants.

71.

They seem to enjoy mixing drinks. For example, their beloved cola/orange soft drink, alternately known as Spezi, Schwip Schwap or Mezzo Mix. And the truly excellent Apfelschorle, apple juice and sparkling water. And why stop at white wine spritzers when you can have a red wine spritzer?

72.

In keeping with this, Germans enjoy mixing beer – with cola, pear, lime or pretty much any other fruit juice. Which, for a nation famed for its superior beer production, is somewhat unexpected.

73.

They seem to be distrustful of any beverage that doesn't sparkle and, despite having excellent tap water, relegate it to second best beneath the bottled, sparkling stuff.

74.

Germans like buying drinks in six packs of 1.5l bottles that are then dutifully recycled, bottle by bottle.

75.

It is extremely rare to see a German throw out a recyclable bottle and, if they do (in the midst of a brain-snap) someone passing by the rubbish bin will very quickly pull the bottle out and take it to the recycling automat themselves.

76.

During large events (festivals, summer grilling bonanzas) there will be people making serious money by collecting revellers' beer bottles.

77.

Germans are (justifiably) concerned about

their online privacy. It is a rare German indeed who uses their full name on Facebook as opposed to a bizarre cross section of their first and last names, for example: Mo Na Berg or Le Na.

78.

Germans have this... thing... with bureaucracy.

79.

Germans extract a curiously large amount of pleasure from the acts of giving, receiving and processing paperwork. They revel in it. Photocopy it. Sign it. Photocopy it again. Roll in it. Cover themselves with it and inhale the scent of paper.

80.

Those who work for the German government seem to... never work at all. It's like their entire system is efficient enough to work by itself, without humans doing anything except photocopying and stamping things.

81.

Germany loves a public holiday. Bavaria in particular.

82.

The whole country quivers with excitement every New Year's Eve when they sit down and watch Dinner for One. But the supremely odd thing isn't a national obsession with a black and white sketch comedy, directed by and starring Brits, that has nothing to do with New Year's Eve, but the fact that this is the one film the Germans don't dub.

83.

They are bizarrely superstitious about wishing people a Merry Christmas too early, opening presents early and celebrating birthdays early.

84.

Should you not have a garden, but yearn for one, you can rent a small square of land called a Kleingarten (small garden). Here you can cultivate a garden and sit back and enjoy the fruits of your labours by resting in a little hut.

85.

The average German garden, big or small, seems unable to resist the lure of the garden gnome. There is almost always one, lurking sinisterly beneath a bush, or partaking in some sort of Mise-en-scène with other concrete characters and a perfectly-clipped shrub.

86.

Germans. Love. Football. Love it. In fact the most passionate you will ever see a German is when they are watching, talking about, thinking about, dreaming about or playing, football.

87.

You may also catch a German in an act of passion if you raise the topic of cars. Germans love their cars and are very proud of their ability to make such good ones. Just ask them.

88.

It is a good thing they have good cars and an Autobahn of terrifying speed because Deutsche Bahn is Germany's dirty little inefficient secret.

89.

Most Germans seem to always buy or possess the appropriate public transport tickets, even though there are so many occasions upon which they could get away with not having one. This sense of honesty will eventually rub off on you.

90.

Germans largely respect "Quiet Time" on Sundays, when they don't vacuum, use lawn mowers or other loud appliances and generally keep noise levels to a bare minimum. In some parts, an unspoken evening Quiet Time is enforced, via disapproval or neighbourly note-leaving.

91.

Church bells are exempt from all Quiet Times.

92.

As ingrained in the German psyche as Quiet Time on Sunday, is the weekly viewing of crime show Tatort...

93.

...and when Tatort isn't on, a German can be found with his or her head buried in a crime novel.

94.

Germans seem to enjoy camping and driving campervans through Europe.

95.

They are inordinately proud of their states, districts, district-free cities, city states, regions, sub-regions, dialects, entirely different vocabularies, sub-cultures, traditions, festivals and basically being really different from the 10-house village that is 5km away because that village is in an entirely different region and therefore nothing like this village.

96.

Germans simply simply love celebrating.

97.

And dressing up.

98.

And that dastardly Schlager music which they all know the words to.

99.

Often all three passions are combined at an inexplicable pop-up festival that features, without exception, the following: medieval beer stalls, a Pommes stand and a wagon with a dazzling array of sugared nuts, waffles and chocolate-covered baked goods.

100.

Generally speaking, Germans are extremely hospitable.

101.

Because of all this, Germans make loyal, warm, lifelong friends.

Afterword

In November 2010, we fled London for Berlin, carrying nothing but a one-way ticket, a suitcase and a cat each. In between assembling impressive winter wardrobes, retraining our livers and negotiating the German bureaucratic labyrinth, we found time to start what is now one of Berlin's biggest English-language blogs: überlin.

In its first three years of existence, überlin has been featured on the front page of The Guardian website, on The Scotsman online and NPR's Berlin Stories blog, and in the pages of British Airways' and Brussels Airlines' in-flight magazines.

Every month, tens of thousands of visitors read überlin to find out what it's really like to live as an expat in Germany. Our website offers valuable advice on relocating, finding a job and settling here, and suggests loads of awesome stuff to do when people move to or visit Berlin.

To get a taste of expat life, and to find out what it is about Germany that continues to enthrall (and tickle) us, visit www.uberlin.eu

Liebe aus Berlin!

Zoë and James
überlin

www.epubli.de